the rising and the rain

the rising and the rain

poems by john straley

University of Alaska Press
Fairbanks, Alaska

University of Alaska Press
P.O. Box 756240
Fairbanks, AK 99775-6240

ISBN 978-1-60223-033-0

Library of Congress Cataloging-in-Publication Data

Straley, John, 1953–
  The rising and the rain : poems / by John Straley.
     p. cm.
  ISBN 978-1-60223-033-0 (pbk. : alk. paper)
  1. Northwest, Pacific—Poetry. 2. Alaska—Poetry. I. Title.
  PS3569.T687R57 2008
  811'.54—dc22
                              2008027541

Cover by Anne Coray
Book design by Paula Elmes

For Curtis Edwards:

who was there at the beginning.

contents

six epithalamions and a birth announcement

the rising and the rain

tennakee springs: september 2001

After the rain we walked the path out of town,
past gardens running along the inlet:
onions, and squash,
pea pods climbing fences
next to a spray of lavender where the woman
I was walking with ran her hands
through the sparklers of blue
then smelled the scented raindrops on her fingers.

We talked about walking out to the point
through alders and onto the flats
where the big animals drag salmon from the river
and leave torn gills
scattered like roses
in circles of flattened grass.

But after three steps,
with our pants wet in the underbrush,
we turned around and decided
to pick red huckleberries all the way back,
putting them one by one
into her drinking cup
like red pearls, until it was so full she
had to walk slowly,

almost on tiptoe,
as if she were balancing all of her good fortune,
and mine, in her lovely,
scented fingers.

words overheard at elmer fudd's funeral

Of course we all laughed at him,
fool that he was;
the big baby head and short legs,
and of course we sided with the black duck
who kissed him hard enough to pull his lips
a foot from his face.
He plodded, hunted
and plodded, was the butt
of all our jokes.

But I miss him so much,
for who could stand to be the straight man
in a world that's hooting
and hopping on its head?
Who carries the shotgun we can plug
with just our two fingers?

We live with a loony kind of irony now,
stuffing dynamite into our own pants
and when we paint the mouth of a tunnel onto that brick wall
we wait
and wait,
and wait,
but no train comes,
so we charge off
and smash into the bricks so hard our
teeth jar loose,
yellow birds circle our heads
singing their sad songs about mortality
and it just doesn't seem so funny anymore.

my sexual legacy

As a boy my father had rolled under trains
and swung up on the slow-moving cars
to hoot and throw stones into the Nowood river.
He drove a Model T Ford to piano lessons in Tensleep
and he slicked his dark hair back with tonic
so he'd look like Valentino.
A ten-year-old sheik, he waited for the trains
in the station house where he lived
and would run errands for the black porters
bringing them cigarettes and matches
if they asked.

He hadn't been circumcised and when it
became infected at age ten, he thought
he had caught venereal disease
from touching himself so he told no one.
But when his mother discovered the blood on his pants
she scolded him for an hour while the doctor
found his way to the station house in the dark,
where he performed the procedure
with a sharp knife, on the kitchen table:
slicing off the tip and
packing the offending penis in ice.

Of course he made up many stories
and I don't know the truth of them now,
but sitting by his bed from which
we both knew he would never rise
we leaned in,
listening for the rumble
of steel wheels
and I could see
he was thinking of something.
"What?" I asked and he looked over to me.
"More sex," he said. "You need more sex in your stories."

wile e. coyote considers the obvious

There seem to be countless routes
to my well-planned failures:
I really thought the rocket
shoes would work.

And the anvil carried across the chasm
on the tightwire rope
seemed reasonable at the time
but now, I wonder?

I lay in bed this morning
my ears bent, my knees swollen
knowing that He was out there but
thinking maybe I shouldn't go.

Maybe I should stay in bed
all day long and read a book
or listen to the news on the radio
but truthfully, I am not meant for that.

Too much introspection is bad for a coyote
and besides, my wife doesn't want me around
tapping my toes, fidgeting with the dynamite
and alarm clocks, the birdseed and suction cups.

She says I have to go
that God must have given me this desire
for some good reason, even if only
to provoke his remote, unfathomable laughter.

"And what do we get?" she says. "We get the ability
to take a punch and become uncrumpled
with every flattening. We can fall through the air
all our lives and land virtually unhurt.

"And besides, what would you do if you caught him?
Such a skinny bird, could not feed you through this
long, unknowable life we blunder through
day by day by day."

on the day they buried gus hall

It was raining on the Iron Range,
and the candidates were practicing for their debates.
I was overstuffed with tropical fruit; lying on my couch
not worried about anything
particularly.
If anyone was dying on the West Bank it didn't matter much
or if the sailors blown to smithereens for some reason
or another had anything to do with me
I didn't really know.

But on the day they buried Gus Hall,
it was raining on the Iron Range,
and the *New York Times* noted that he had been wrong
about almost everything,
from the workers revolution
to vacationing in North Korea.

He had big hands they said, "like a lumberjack,"
had pumped iron in Leavenworth,
was befriended by Machine Gun Kelly
and had loved one woman all of his life.
"Unreconstructed" the *Times* called him.

That night I turned on the candidates' debate,
and while they sprayed, and sprayed
each other's legs
I ate another mango and dreamed of the Iron Range
where the clouds move like
Soviet-style combines churning ice out of the sky
and Gus Hall is out there somewhere
lying silent as a fallen tree
while the termites underfoot, continue their life's work
and take their first little nibbles of his coffin
for no one else's profit,
other than their own.

the new year

Last night I was
lying on my stomach
with my head cradled in my hands
listening to a Louis Prima album,
when I looked up and saw my mother
standing in the doorway
so thin and white she could have been
a banner of vapor lifting past a street lamp.
"I'm sorry," I said. "Was the music too loud?"
"Oh no, honey," she said,
her voice as calm as melted wax.
"I just can't stay here anymore."
And when she hugged me I knew then she was dead.
I smelled her hand lotion fading
and the delicate bones up and down her back
crumbled under my hands.
Then we dissolved into a column of steam
and rose into the air, both of us, faithless and serene
leaving not a trace of anything behind
except a slight fog on the windows
which was already clearing
as the stylus scratched at the end of the record
going around, and around, and around.

for a boy who has to write a poem for school

Imagine a raven
at your bedroom window.
Forget your assignment
and put the pencil down.
The bird will cock his head
this way
and that,
until he lifts away
leaving that empty,
bobbing branch
to write
everything
you need to say.

not anymore

Headed north.
I am knee-scabbed and sore
from working on this boat,
cracking wrenches on the red Ford engines
floating, swearing, floating
until I look up and I'm on the far side of the Queen Charlottes
where the breeze brings the scent of cedar
off the mud-slipped bluffs
and somehow the engines start to hum.

In Seattle my brother
keeps our parents' ashes in the bottom of his closet.
Before leaving he asked if I wanted them.
"No," I said.

There are dead trees, gray and slick
spinning in the quick currents near shore,
some of the hillsides are bare,
some of the villages are empty
but the currents run their consistent
push-pull circuit of the moon.

"No," I said, "you keep them, and someday
we'll find a place where they belong.
We'll all put up a plaque or something
and that will be it."
"Be careful," he said giving me a hug good-bye.
"There are many ways to get lost up there,"
and I said right back,
"But not for me, not as many at least,
not anymore."

Late in the day pulling into Bella Bella
an old man in a canvas coat
was rowing a wooden dory south
with his black dog in the stern.
I couldn't see him clearly,
but I think he set his drink down
to consider me.
The wind and currents were fair for him.
He waved as if we were old friends
and then, without thinking,
I waved back.

what i wouldn't give for this

In the library, the drunk
who usually sleeps with his dogs
snoozes with a copy of *Guns and Ammo* on his chest

while the girl next to him
listens to music through her headphones;
the Brandenburg Concertos leaking into the room.

Through the windows the alder trees have scarfs of snow
wrapping around their papery bark,
and the storm makes whitecaps on the Sound.

I may waste the entire day in the library
reading magazines about boat building
or collecting vintage guitars

or the various recipes for berry cobbler
or how to stitch a pinwheel quilt
or what dessert to make for friends losing weight.

I'll read anything
but the newspapers
with the body count for the day.

I won't read the corespondents' reports
or the angry opinion pieces, I won't look
at the sad-eyed soldiers rumbling down those dusty roads.

I'll sit by the window
until the slush ball of the sun flares
into a gray-green sea

and the drunk puts back his magazine
then shambles outside to where his dogs are tied
and wanders off down the street;

all of those skinny dogs barking
and nipping at his feet
happy to see him, once again

so warm, and so safe.

dark green

*"Either I've always spoken from the heart
in situations like this, or I never had
and don't know what it means."*
—*Enduring Love* by Ian McEwan

Late summer.
There are so many things I want to tell you
but just as I put my thoughts together
another whale comes to the surface.

You lift your camera
and time narrows
into that moment when the animal lifts
its flukes then disappears with her
heart as big as a spruce stump
beating somewhere beneath us.

The sun slants down,
a milky light rises from
the gray-green sea.

Whales rise to the surface
exhaling, inhaling
pushing away
from our thin buoyancy
back into the dark green
of everything
I am trying to say.

the enthusiasts

The ground was so full of old bones
the boys tried sleeping
standing up,
listening to the whippoorwill
calling between
the creaking harnesses
and swinging butt chains
of draft horses
pulling cannons into place.

The darkness came up from the ground
like those bones of the soldiers
they were camped upon: skulls
and rib cages kicked up each time
someone tried to dig a hole
or scour a new pad for a tent.

They were near Chancellorsville
where General Lee had claimed a victory
that cost him twenty percent of his army
and the boys made grim jokes
trying to distance themselves
from the next morning when, they knew,
it would happen
all over again.

This was the business of the day.
And when that morning came
the horses from each side whinnied
across the opening, and those boys
stood up straight, shook themselves
then walked into the clearing
where seven thousand of them died
in a little more than an hour.

Look down on us stars
there is nothing left of them now.
Today men scour the ground
with metal detectors,
and fat horses pull cannons
into place for the re-enactment,
while the bees continue
to work the wildflowers
with their sickening
sound and one
enthusiast
in a period costume
reads a list of names,
while the whippoorwill sing, the sun sets
and nobody dies
right then
right there.

respite

for Gary—on his birthday
May 8, 2003

Spring comes
and on the porch our caged bird sings
tunes to the crows perched
above him in the alders
while someone talks about the brown bear
being killed up the hill after he ate
the veterinarian's old yellow dog
and the seniors in high school skip
their afternoon classes to drink warm beer
in their pickups out past the turn-around.

I suppose I should be worried
but I can't seem to muster the concern.

Let them all rest now:
the faithful old dog,
our vain yellow bird,
the dopey young bear,
and the high school seniors.
Let them fold themselves up in this
promise the earth always keeps,
and let them rest
for this spring is brief
and those final tests
were never worth taking anyway.

fire camp

Years ago now, I worked in the Cascade range
running a packstring up the side hills
taking supplies to the fire crews.
Thinking I was just headed up
for the day the fireboss shook my hand
and gave me a paper sleeping bag
to lay out on the ledge above camp.

I turned out the string in the meadow
with a bell and hobbles on the mare,
the mouse brown mules watching her every move,
skittery around the smell of smoke.
The fire just a haze of light
like a small town behind the hill: a few thin
sparks zagging upwards, and burning out of sight,
while I slept in my crackling bag.

I was up before dawn, stumbling towards the bell
the nightsong of the crickets still echoing
in that cold morning of another hot day
and when I found the mare, she swung
her anvil head towards the grain
I pretended to carry in my hat and
lunged her two cuffed front legs
over the rocky ground
to come to me.

I turned 16 on that fire
complained about being there then
and now I complain of other things:
my knees, and joints, the sleepiness
that overcomes me some afternoons.
But sometimes before the sun breaks
over the hill, I can still hear the ringing
of that bell mare in the meadow
during my first fire season
when I knew for certain
I was alive.

every single day

(After Raymond Carver's Hummingbird*)*

Suppose I said the word "springtime"
and I wrote the words "king salmon"
on a piece of paper
and mailed it to you.
When you opened it
would you remember that afternoon we spent
together in the yellow boat
when the early whales were feeding
and we caught our first fish of the year?

Or would you remember that time off Cape Flattery
when you were a little girl:
your father smoking, telling stories as he ran the boat,
then the tug and zing of that very first fish
spooling off into the gray-green world;
you laughing and brushing back your hair
before setting the hook?

I know I am hard to understand sometimes
particularly when you are standing
at the post office with only a piece of paper
saying "king salmon" on it
but just think of it as a promissary note
and that electric tug, that thrill
pulling your mind into deep water
is how I feel about you every,
single day.

what god, glenn gould, and the heron on my beach must have in common

The ocean is breathing on the cobbled beach
and a heron yawps out from under the dark pilings.
In my office Glenn Gould is playing the Goldberg Variations
through the tiny speakers of my secondhand player.
I hear him groan and tap his foot as if he wanted
all the notes, the whole world, to come out all at once
in one layered gasp.
This must be the exquisite pain
which comes from creating something
as beautiful as mortality.

The gulls fly by in the dark and when they rise to the fluorescent lamps
they glow like space ships, vivid
as a waking dream,
vivid as that last memory of my mother's hair
under her bedside lamp.

Glenn Gould plays to the end, then stops.
The heron disappears into the dark
but through the window I still hear it calling out,
"Hey! Hey! Hey I'm still here."

rules of war

On March 30, 2003 an American soldier
discharged his weapon into
a van which was trying to crash
his checkpoint a hundred miles from Baghdad.

After the van stopped
and the nervous soldiers pulled open
the riddled door,
the bodies of women and children
tumbled out like entrails.

Everyone talks about the rules of war
when there is really only one:
once the killing starts
you open your arms to death
and hug it, like a stranger
who comes to your door
in his overcoat,
and you cling to him so hard
you can't let go
until the last person
who is supposed to die, decides, "Not today,"
and the soldier about to shoot
says the same,
then the war is over:
the stranger takes off his coat,
sits down in your living room
and you have to live with him
the rest of your life.

your first snow

for Cora Grace Dow
Born: 11/27/01

On the day you were born
all the news concerned
the calamitous end of things:
banks of clouds came in from the west
and voices on the radio grew thin
in the upper atmosphere.
The wind tumbled pieces of Christmas ribbon
down the sidewalk and a gray cat
slapped at the glass
hissing.

But that first night on Jeff Davis Street
your parents watched you sleep, thankful
that it was only rain falling on the roof
and ravens standing guard on the wires
running down the quiet street,
and when the snow started to fall
trees wrapped themselves in pillows of it.

Your mother curled you
under her coat and took you to where
trumpeter swans paddled
in the green eddies of Indian River:
birds with noisy necks arching like question marks
pushed against the current,
and when the wind blew
snow sizzled off the spruce limbs
drawing a white curtain across the river,
across these visiting angels
swimming in green
and even on the radio,
the talkers stopped talking about the war
and stood by
in the hushed presence
of everything
you were born into.

poem for october

I have turned off the radio.
The voices from a long way off call for storms
but already my small float house is knocking
against the tarry pilings
and the gangway is giving away.
All weekend I spent tacking down
a neighbor's roof and laying in
enough supplies for my friends and family:
water, chocolate, rice and cheese
enough firewood and batteries
for the foreseeable future.
Later I will tape the windows
and put plastic over all the books,
but for a moment I stand outside
and listen to the loose corner of my own roof
shrieking in the gusts.
The wind is filled with a blustery energy
while across the bay the glittering clouds
carry bits of broken glass
churning over the mountain passes
scything their way to low ground.

Everything is alive now:
Hector has not been drug behind the chariot
and Lincoln is readying himself for the play.
Millions of the forgotten, sprawled out
like broken dolls on the battlefields of the world,
pick themselves up
and dust themselves off
only to ask each other
"Brother, where have we been?"
But they do not hug
nor go inside
because they know that soon enough
they will be dead again.

mid-winter miracle

I'm told that this is a new year
but it feels like just another winter morning.
The thin membrane of the moment
is held in place by cold air
and I still cannot see into the future.
Instead, I dreamed I was standing beside
a green river and tried to cross
to the other side where my wife was waiting,
laughing as if she couldn't quite figure out
how we got to be separated.
There were tall towers built on each bank
but no span between, so looking to make
some kind of progress
I climbed straight up into the air,
climbing until my arms burned
thinking I was getting closer to her when
I wasn't, so I stopped; looked down
where the river was now just a line
and my beautiful wife a distant abstraction.
I began bicycling my left leg into the empty air,
trying to find that lateral step
which had never been there.

All of the water in the river
was whispering, "Stay where you are,"
then I asked, "But for how long?" and I got no answer
because I remembered that the river was frozen
so, when I woke up, I squandered
the forty new seconds of daylight
rubbing my eyes
thinking there wasn't much hope
of this being a short winter
until I reached across the bed
where my living wife was sleeping,
under a tangle of quilts
as warm and as fragrant
as spring.

in this dream about love

We are driving across the western states
on the back roads
past small towns with grain elevators
and the last three years spray-painted
on the lone water tower.

It is late summer,
school about to begin
and we pull over to watch
the high-school football team practice:
farm boys in ragged workout uniforms
battering each other and catching passes.
Alongside of the field a pretty white girl
laces her fingers through the galvanized fencing
watching the boys play.
Her books are scattered behind her
and she looks as if she has been crying.
You say that you don't ever want to be young again
and I agree then we drive to the tavern
to drink a beer and watch the weather on TV
where there are clouds and patches of sun
and wind that will not blow
as fast as our car can drive.

As the locals come in after work
they turn the music up and
look at us suspiciously
then we buy them a drink and they
loosen up, ask about our car,
where we're going and you say
that we are in love so they buy us a round,
and we leave.

As we pull out the pretty white girl from the field
is walking by herself towards the Dairy Queen
but she looks happy now
and you wave as we accelerate out of town.
Then you tell me you really do love me
and wasn't just saying that so they would buy us a drink.
I say I'm glad of that
and don't you think it would be all right
if we stay somewhere nice tonight?
Then you become a red-tailed hawk
hopping easily out the open window

landing high up on a phone wire
in strange flat light because
by now the sun is a snowball
behind a wind-smeared cloud.
I pull over and call and call to you.
I even hold out my arm
giving you a place to alight
but you won't come down.

after simone weil

Like a confused lover
I waited for you
on the wrong corner,
looking at my watch, each moment
confirming our missed appointment.

The unsubstantial business of the world,
the empty buses and garbage trucks,
whirled like mists
around my immovable heart.

I imagined you waiting for me
somewhere
holding steadfast in your faith.
Not calling the police,
not wanting me
to appear foolish.

"How you must love me," I thought,
"to make us both wait so long."

one sided

On the day after you killed yourself
we spoke over the phone.
You said it wasn't over,
this life you thought
you could turn off
like a light.

You said you're stuck near a phone
with my number scratched in the paint
and all you can do is talk to me
without even changing your clothes,
stiff as meat wrappers
with your own blood.

I thought of saying how much I hated you
for that pitiless betrayal,
that turning away,
but I wanted to hear your voice again
so I stayed on.

You wouldn't let me say a thing;
you talked and talked
but in the pauses
when I heard your breathing
on the end of the line,
I remembered the autumn
we stood on the precipice
above the crushed-shell beach
and the wind took our voices away
into that immaculate distance
where there is always room enough,
where there is always time enough.

You started to justify yourself and I hung up.
There is nothing I want to hear from you now.
At night I take the receiver off the hook
but when I sleep, I hear you dialing,
doing everything in your power
to get through.

ain't that a man?

This morning Muddy Waters sits
cross-legged on a short-napped carpet
in the shed behind his house
feebly trying to empty his mind.
Eyes set on the middle distance,
ears picking up every thread
of sound being woven through the air:
a Swainson's Thrush
on the phone line near the road,
a speedboat sputtering and lunging across the lake.
A wind-up clock ticking on the desk.

His favorite thing to do
when he wasn't playing his red guitar
or making love to some young woman
or another
was to lie on his black leather couch
eating black walnut ice cream
and grape Nehi all smooshed up together.

"Now ain't that a man,"
the blues man thinks to himself,
"Swainson's Thrush
Ticking clock,
black walnut ice-cream
and grape soda
all smooshed up together?"

first kiss

We sat by the fire until everyone went to their tents
and when she kissed me I didn't
know where to put my shaking hands.
The fire sizzled and the wind
clacked the limbs together.
She laughed and kissed me again
then stood up to lie down in her tent
while I crept off to sleep on the saddle pads
near the sweat-soaked tack
to keep the salt-crazed deer away.

In the morning the brown gelding I had kept in
stomped the hard ground
snuffling for bits of grain near the overturned pan.
The bells from the mares I had turned loose
chimed in the hollow along the edge of the burn
and I put on my pants in a hurry.

I went into her tent
and kissed her again,
and this time she took my cold
hands, aching from a summer of
bucking her father's hay
and slipped them under
her flannel nightshirt.

Off the edge of the ridge
a black bear shambled into the clearing
sending the startled mares up the hill
their bells clanging,
legs pounding the frozen ground
with their great hearts racing
straight into the morning.

ghost dance

for Alfredo Vea Jr.

That morning you got out of bed before
the sunlight found its way to the pavement,
getting ready for your day in court defending
the boys born to be contract killers.

You stood by your screen door watching
the light work its way down the red tile roofs
while the palm trees a block away
began glowing in that syrupy light
which comes with the day still
belonging to the small birds
slipping through the morning
speaking the only language they will ever know
saying to themselves "water" and "daylight";
saying "fear,"
and you remember
that nothing we can wear will make us bulletproof
no matter how hard we listen or wait for
our Grandfathers to come back. There is no hat
to look under and see all the animals who have
been wasted across the plains towards Kansas.
We live in a huge and forgetful country
where Wovoka the Paiute prophet outlived
all those women and children
buried in the frozen ditch
at Wounded Knee.
He ended up living until 1932
and worked as an extra in the silent movies:
the stoic Indian in the tall black hat.

But even then he knew
the weight in your heart
as you drove across the bridge from Oakland
to begin your day in lockup
he even wrote it down in a letter
to the Indian territories:
"Do not tell the white people," he said,
"the dead are still alive again,
I do not know when they will be here;
maybe this fall
or in the spring."

baby on a girder

for Lee and Morced

Remember the baby in peril cartoons?
In that peach-colored atmosphere
if adults appeared at all they were only the shapely legs
of mothers with high heels and seams running up their stockings
and the fathers' voices were simply braying bassoons with no earthly
    authority.
The big-headed baby living in a skyscraper somewhere
wakes up cooing and burbling from his bed
then without a moment of hesitation steps out the window.
We gasp for an instant and wonder at the senselessness of all this
just as the crane swings the girder past and the baby crawls along its
    edge
from one improbable disaster to the next, as horns blare,
anvils fall, fat tired cars rumble past like buffaloes
and pianos dangle from frayed ropes . . .

But all the while the baby burbles under his bonnet
knees bumping inside his dressing gown,
oblivious in a too blue sky,
immune, it seems from gravity.

Watching it now we may want to tie the baby down,
or wrap him in padding head to toe,
make a plan, for God's sake.
But children know the truth.
They know the baby in peril cartoon
is not about gravity, flesh, and bone
but is only a small hand-drawn parable,
of our soul's own journey,
and we knew it too,
standing at the curb
reaching up for our mother's hand
whether we wanted to or not
or later, as parents ourselves, when we wrapped the toddler in a
    scratchy towel
pulling him back from the waves breaking on the sand

scanning the horizon for the fins of sharks,
that were probably not there
but still . . .
And we know the truth now, when our children go off on their own and
    we are sick with worry
but we release them just the same because this freedom is the gift
    we've been working on
like a Christmas present late at night, for all of the days of their lives,
and even though we know the world is fraught with danger
there is nothing to do but let them go.

The baby coos as it crawls into the bull ring and shakes its red rattle in
    the air,
and when the insane red-eyed monster rages and batters through the
    dirt
we are not startled when a great bird swoops down
and plucks the laughing baby from the earth.

Just as that peach-colored sunlight begins to fade,
and the world below thins into a murmur of distant horns,
the drowsy baby settles back down into his bed,

and the story ends,
regardless of how much we are loved
or what age we are chosen to become
we settle into the final scene
safe and without pain,
perfect once again
and at peace.

the erotic life of books

Did you know that inside a computer
there is no such thing as touch?
There are endless numbers and codes;
the "yes" "no"s of almost everything
we can possibly imagine,
but no real rubbing together.

Books in the library though,
touch one another.
They lean there in orderly
yet lovely, uneven rows
with well-thumbed covers
snuggled tight.
Take one out too fast and you can hear
a sighing.

You can smell their breath
back in the stacks,
those old books, musty and unread
waiting next to the glossy bestsellers.
They smell like leather
and dust, those old ones,
and when you open one
you can hear a soft moan,
"Thank you," they say.

No wonder we learn to flirt in the library.
Walking with a fingertip down their spines:
Herodotus and Heaney and Hirshfield and Hogan,
the bodies of their work right here
under the skin.

We go to the back
past row after row of books,
a hundred million actual words
there, between sheets,
bound in leather, and linen
and old thick cardboard worn to velvet.
We slip a note to the stranger,
reading in the last carrel
right up to closing time.
"I am really here," the note says,
"I have proof."

happy stories

After the funeral an old Aunt
sat with her sister, their punch cups
teetering on the edge of an uneven card table.
"You knew, Thomas died of a heart attack just three years ago?
He wouldn't listen to Enid about eating all that fat but what would you
    expect from
a hard-headed Finn?" They shook their heads
like twin pendulums ticking off the seconds.
Sun slanted in through the garden windows,
kids chased each other in some wild game or another, their laughter
feeling like fresh rain as one sister tried to top the other.
"Well, Betsy died falling down her cellar stairs looking
for a jar of peaches, and Carl just kept calling after her
complaining that the ice cream was getting warm."
The women chuckled, as a kid sprinted into the room
clutching someone else's hat
spilling the juice, upsetting the dog
and causing the cat to arch and spit.
"But you knew Alice died of a brain hemorrhage right there in Hawaii,"
the Aunt said daubing at the lurid red stain on the front of her dress.
"In her new bathing suit, no less."

The kids wrestled in the flowerbeds now. Uncles swearing
dogs snarling, but the Aunts wouldn't stop talking about grisly death.
Each one trying to top the other as if they would eventually come to
    that final,
and most absurd dying anyone could imagine.
A death so ridiculous that we would laugh until we couldn't
laugh, until our sides would swell and our skin stretch tight
over heaving lungs,
laugh so hard we would rise right out of our chairs
and float away from the house
leaving the casseroles and the adder mouthed flowers, in silence,
our hilarity growing thin in the upper atmosphere,
for these Aunts only want to find that one story about death
so absurdly funny

we could circle the heavens on the richness of it
like a satellite preserved in orbit
forever
and ever.

But they couldn't, so we sat plopped in our chairs
and ate the ham, washed off the children when they came in
then tried to tell any old story,
until the dishes were put away
and it was finally time to go,
with one foot in front of the other,
tethered here firmly
to the surface of the earth.

pepe le pew's tristia

You think I don't know you are a cat,
that this passion of mine is somehow misinformed
as if a stripe down the back from a dripping paint can
could obscure the truth of you, and misdirect my ardor.

You think I don't know how I affect you
how the smell of me makes you weak with disgust
as if I didn't see your eyes widen with horror as I come through
the opening of my own arms, kissing the air, pledging my undying
    love.

But my darling, God made skunks passionate
precisely because we smell so bad.
We can barely stand ourselves
and this is why we fall in love with the wrong cats.

My doctor says this is unhealthy.
I do not care, for this is my exquisite tristia
to kiss the air where you once were
to say your name over and over again, insistently.

But here is the truth of it: all my life I have loved mistakenly
for love is the only mistake a true skunk must keep on making.

finding lou

It was early spring, sleet fell on old snow
and I needed to find a fisherman named Lou.
I'd heard he'd seen a bar fight almost a year ago
but he wasn't answering my calls, so
I walked to the swimming pool to sit in the bleachers
with a book I knew I wouldn't read
and watched dozens of slick-skinned children
slide back and forth, through the chlorinated water.

I found my only son, slippery and pink,
rolling along in his lane as if he were a manatee,
dreaming through his warm, clean world;
dreaming through the expanse of chlorinated water,
while on the other side of the walls
sleet glazed the town, and the icy mounds
of old snow were sinking down
revealing dog turds and discarded sandwich boxes thrown down
      months ago.

Up in the hills brown bears were dreaming in their dens of slick fat
salmon, and starved-down carcasses of snow-trapped deer.
But in the forced air of the junior high school building,
mothers and fathers sat in the bleachers watching,
some were laughing and others reading through
newsletters, or fumbling with stubs from checks they'd written.
I asked Norm if he'd seen Lou, and he shook his head
but said Lou might have been up to the bar around three o'clock.

I stepped through the steam
to hurry my son so we could walk down to the street.
He dresses quickly, my good luck. Ten years old and will still walk
with me in public but as I hold his hand crossing the street
he wiggles free and I feel the heat from the shower on his palm,
and smell the chlorine on his damp skin.
Hail fell, striking like frozen peas, and the street
became a frantic rubble of white, before turning to sleet.

I walked and thought of getting done with this case
and maybe looking at the short listings of State jobs.
My son was not speaking but walking beside me

dreaming those questioning dreams of his:
What does "inflammable" mean? Who is Demi Moore?
What happens when people die?
His mind ticking like a combine along the furrows
of the blue-black universe.

The barmaid asked what I wanted and I told her I wasn't drinking
then asked if she had seen Lou
and could I get some change for my kid
so he could play some games.
She said, "Don't let him get wild," and I said,
"Fuck you . . . get wild. This is my kid, Katie. Give me bourbon and
    water,"
and she did, then nodded to her left where Lou was sitting like
a broken fencepost at the bar.

All Lou could remember were some skippers pushing and swearing,
someone spitting, and a couple of cheap shots to the rib cage.
When it moved out on the sidewalk Lou didn't follow, why should he?
The fight hadn't made much of an impression
for it wasn't until hours later someone found the older guy
with his leg broken, his face split up the middle,
lying down on the docks where no one was dancing
and the gulls were hee hawing their laughter in the dark.

"Fights. Hell I've seen fights,"
Lou said, but he hadn't seen the blood
or the bone pushing up against the old man's pants leg,
and a year later, Lou was sitting here drinking, and laughing,
in the same bar where my son was shooting down
space ships and Katie was talking to a regular
who could barely find his mouth with a cigarette.
I drank my drink and thought who was I kidding about getting a State
    job.

The cold rain fell all around the bar
while Lou was telling me how sorry he was,
and Katie leaned back to ask
if I wanted anything else and I said,
No I had to go home so I could get some sleep
and she said, "You'll have plenty of time for sleep when you're dead,"
then the regular bought me another drink,
while my son rattled and kacked at the alien ships.

This is how life goes:
We dream and cross each other's dreams like the ripples
some raindrops leave.
Sometimes we pay attention but often, not in time.
I sat and drank and forgot about Lou
or the State job, or the swimming pool.
I cashed a check while darkness crept like steam around the windows
and the rain kept slicing down.

Finally I had to go, so I called his mother to come get us,
and although she wasn't happy, she said she would.
Waiting there, I held my son's hand and I told him this:
"Up in the hills the bears are not really sleeping,
but they live in an uneasy torpor,
and I think this is the way God wants it
to protect his most dangerous mammals
from killing one other."

Then he smiled at me sweetly
as if he could see the great blue planet
glittering like a raindrop falling through the dark
and he asked me for another quarter.

my heart went boom

Last night, during the fifth-grade play
the little girl playing Titania
grimaced through her lines
saying, *"Come, sit thee down upon this flow'ry bed,*
While I thy amiable cheeks do coy" as if
the donkey-headed kid playing
Nick Bottom was covered in shit.
But still, we all laughed,
and clapped our hands sore
when the poor shadows bowed and hammed it up
for their many curtain calls.

"I'm like that," I told my wife,
as we walked across the parking lot.
"What, like Nick Bottom?" she asked.
"No, like a kid reciting his lines in
a play he doesn't understand."
She smiled then stroked my ugly ears.
"No you're not," she said
and the wind pushed through the lot
sending the electrical wires above our car
swaying crazily from their poles
as if to remind me
that each moment,
every single one,
is almost more than
I bargained for.

for bill, lost at sea

There are no new stories about you anymore,
frozen in time as you've become.
A tarantula trapped in plastic, bought at a Mexican
roadside store, my memories of you
have been put away,
and I don't dig them out
without a few drinks first.

Down at the Pioneer Bar
I lift a glass
and say your name
a proper noun,
somehow in the past tense now,
saying it as if it were a souvenir
and you were standing nearby,
just outside
pulling up your hood
and on your way to that other home,
for which I have no name
and no keepsakes.

walking back

On this day in November
I awoke in the familiar darkness
dressed in my oldest clothes.
My rifle was by the door.
The canvas knapsack packed
the night before.
I knew without thinking,
I needed to walk beyond my house
past the call of the neighbor's dog
so I could shake off the broken glass
of last night's arguments.

The grass beside the road was frozen
bent in the direction of the wind
subservient and motionless,
as if dead
or at best, secretive.

I walked up the hill
listening to the chomp
of my feet on frosty ground.
"I'm a lazy bastard," I thought
as I always do when I start off alone,
and after an hour and a half
I had risen to the next bench above the house.
I could see the white smoke rise
from the breakfast fires
and my neighbor's wife dancing outside
in her nightgown to pick up
last night's paper.

There was nothing to do
so I sat down.
I ate my lunch
though it wasn't noon
and I loaded my gun.

There is so much in this life
I don't deserve
both good and bad,
but what to make of that?
A raven ate my crust and said
something I couldn't understand.
The sun unfolded frozen grass
moving now, night's back unbent.
The world was yet green and I was getting cold,
so I unloaded my gun
and walked back.

words to say while kissing

I would say "perfect"
then lean into you
tasting your breath
and the salt on your lips.

I'd say "lovely" moving my tongue
lightly onto yours,
laughing as your breath fills
my cheeks.

I would say your name
over and over again
making you more than
lips, or tongue, or breath.

I would say your name
and you would become the cool water of a deep lake
holding both our bodies
above the leaf-matted bottom,
suspended where we could say everything,
every word,
in our skin's
specific vocabulary.

because you asked me what i was thinking on the day i took my son out of school to watch the elders bless a totem your brother so recently started

for Dave Galanin

I was thinking that my great-grandfather had been promised a new life
    in America.
He had been a coal miner in Wales
and after he made the journey across the ocean
they had him back in a dark hole
spitting up bloody soot,
digging the exact same coal.

He hung himself in a silo he was so angry.
Later my grandfather was spared going to jail
for stealing from the railroad
and had to live in that small town,
in the shadow of that silo
where his wife turned a mean face to the world
and his sons learned to forget.
So, unknown to me I had been prepared
for the day when my father woke up crying
and I was turned over to the maid,
told nothing.
Anonymous calls came: voices of reporters asking,
"Your daddy is crazy. Isn't that true, boy?
Your daddy is crazy?"
My only answer was "No . . . " before my mother took the receiver
slammed it down on the desk and walked away.

I was thinking this because I wanted to tell you
even white people have been disappointed in this America.
That promises easily made
are rarely kept:
by anyone.
That the rich may believe they are the owners of this land
but they have no title
and this haunts them,
becoming the subject of all their literature.

I took him from school
to tell him that one story is seldom
wholly true.
That shame is not the subject of our lives
but acts as the darkness at our backs
orienting us forward
toward whatever light there is.

I wanted him to see that light
for himself.
How greatness starts
on a particular day
(called this lucky day)
in a particular place
(called this nearly perfect place)
where the great people
Kiksadi, Coho, Boxhouse, Eagle, Kogwantaan,
and all of their kin,
set their differences aside
to honor their dead
who live all around us
all the time
their faces,
part of this land
part of this sky.

I wanted to tell him
that if we can just observe greatness
maybe he and I
might learn a blessing
not just for the tree
not just for the tools
but for coal
and the corn in the silo
where the frayed rope stands ready.

All we want
is to belong.
For there is no going back,
to Wales, to Africa, to France.
All our dead surround us now
and each child born is coming home
to the land where your people
learned these devotions
and were the first to become fully human
in this particular place
called the universe.

gibberish

for Norm Campbell

If our lives are a story,
of yours I know this:
on a day long ago, you were crouching
near a man who had enjoyed
the work of war
and when a sniper shot him,
and only him,
right straight through the skull
you didn't grieve.

Now we get to be old
and have lives which proceed
like pinballs
bouncing from flipper to flipper
where the lights flash
and we never really
know what we've won
if it's only another chance to play the game:
to paint, and fiddle with words
and walk through the wet woods
looking for a prey that may
or may not be there.

You told me once you couldn't make
out most contemporary poems,
but I think it's really our fate
which is a kind of gibberish:
bullets through the brainpans
and great loves which come unbidden,
none of it makes sense
and all of it is our business.

Let me leave it here:
I'm grateful it wasn't you killed that day
and I almost have to believe
that fate was speaking clearly then
even if it was in a language
we do not understand.

eavesdropping

for Bill Stafford

The river,
        as it passes,
says,
           "See? It's easy,"

but the rain
    wants nothing
        more
than a place to rest.

"Too noisy,"
        is the only thing
the snow says.

the rising and the rain

*for J.P. Seaton and his translation of
Ou-Yang Hsiu's "Love and Time"*

I.

The space I want to enter is not like Death:
a blanket pulled over my head,
or the darkness I fall through on my way to sleep.
The space I want to enter is under the arc
of rising water:
before the rain lifts up from the sea
or the ponds by some lonely inland farm
or the teapot boiling over on that farmer's stove,
or when the Bedouin opens her skin bag to drink
and the world cannot help but enter first
letting that little slip of a storm
whisper out of a cool, dark mouth.

The place I want to enter
sits beside the wood stove
with a stew pot on top
bubbling off the liquid and the wind blows
against the single-pane windows
while I am waiting for a story
to begin.

II.

The storm rolls in from the southwest,
and snow chokes the upper ravines
so that the little stream by the house begins to wither.

I'm making venison stew
cutting up the deer and stirring the pot slowly
wondering why I should worry,

spring always comes,
it always has,
and yet these last few Novembers . . .

When I shot this deer
he fell hard
like a marionette whose strings had been cut.

Now the crows sit above the garden plot
waiting for me to throw out
the scraps of fat I will not use.

I love every inch of this deer I killed
but still the crows must eat,
so I slice between each rib

parsing out one bit for my family
and another for the world
then scatter the scraps on the garden.

Crows startle, then settle on the meat.
When they finish they bicker for a moment
then rise from the turned-under garden and disappear.

All that's left is to cook and eat.
The surge of spring is in the stream
and spring's clouds, like desire, rise . . .

There is nothing to fear
and nothing to care for
but love and time.

III.

A light rain freckles the bay,
where three boats pull
their gear without heeling over.
I watch them all morning
while our black dog
sleeps under my desk.

A letter from a friend says that he is thirsty all the time.
Most of the fighters are bad shots
and many of their mortars are duds.
He's not that impressed with their weapons.
But every day, the old men wave
from their sand-swept stoops while vehicles
loaded with bombs
roll like milk trucks down the streets.
"It's worse than you've heard," he said,
"it's messier."

Here, the alder trees are showing their first sticky buds
and lazy gulls feed on herring eggs.
Yesterday I caught a warm breeze
slinking over the low-tide beach
the one that brought the stink of fish and seaweed.
I watched crows walk the eelgrass beds,
stooping and picking like field hands.

I've heard that in Washington the cherry blossoms
are a haze of pink beside the monuments,
where men and women stop by the coffee carts,
on their way to their offices talking
about restaurants, the war
and what could happen next,
and I imagine the flutter of the wet blossoms
covering parked cars when the storm comes
and when one of them drives away
there is a black space of empty pavement
in the glittering mâché of pink.

A few raindrops fall from leaf to leaf
growing fatter as they near the ground.
My dog gets up and goes outside.
I follow her across the yard.
No one shoots at us.
No mine explodes.
The dust of broken buildings
does not settle like a pall.

The boats pull their nets
with a few silver fish
flopping on their decks,
and our dog circles her bed by the heater
to lay down.

IV.

The space I want to enter is not like Death:
a blanket pulled over my head,
or the darkness I fall through on my way to sleep.
The space I want to enter is under the arc
of rising water: the pot of venison left on the stove,
and all of our bodies along with it
rising up toward the ceiling
through the cracks in the roof
the great condensation of ghosts
blowing across the surface of the earth,
countless individuals dissolving, and reforming
rising in ripples from the desert floor
rising in the shredding clouds up the sides of mountains
rising from bombed-out buildings
and hospital tents hastily strung up
where the living rush back and forth
asking very few questions
but none at all of the dead,
who cannot hear them now
nor take any part in their plans
being busy, as we all are,
with this day to day story
of the rising
and the rain.

overheard in the public defender's waiting room

Let's say one of the Kennedys has to go to court
and their car won't start.
Then they ask their neighbor at ten minutes to nine
if he can give them a ride.
Do you think the neighbor mumbles something
about living with the choices they've made
before he drives off,
kicking gravel up
on the Kennedy's pants leg?

Do you think they just stand there holding
their little kids blubbering in the slush
wondering what to do
while the judge downtown issues
a bench warrant causing the fat-tired
police cars to roll out the road?

I don't know.
Maybe it's true
what all the magazines say;
that the rich have their own
exquisite suffering;
something blue-blooded and fine
like a champagne hangover
that even time won't cure.

But I'd take my fucking chances,
long falls from great heights and all.
The rich aren't just like us.
Their cars start, for one thing,
and even when someone refuses them something
it never sounds like tires
on a frozen gravel road.

satisfied

He had always bragged
that when the time came
he was going to end his life
before accepting that dribbling down
of decrepitude.
There would be none of that undignified slumping,
the club-footed foolishness of old men.

He would jump, or shoot or drug himself
off the stage, keeping that decisive
image of himself alive
like the creased photograph his mother
had secreted in her wallet.

But with each new ache and pain
came promises for the next day:
the slant of light on the tangled garden,
or the way the ravens chimed
up in the woods,
even the taste of hot sauce
on the pale hospital eggs.

When his left side went
and the speech slurred,
he remembered his earlier resolve
and he cast his one good eye around the room
for a sharp tool or an open window . . .
. . . but then . . . there was that song on the radio
and the bristly cool air
through the window held
the promise of another season.

On the last day he refused morphine
and ate his eggs laying flat on his back
trying to roll his eyes to see
what was coming up
so suddenly from behind
"More . . . " he said.
"Just a little more,"
and he was satisfied.

my finest work

Twenty-five years later
we went looking for our cabin site
but there was no trace of the place

where we had spent three winters
reading Russian novels
and playing dominoes in that sooty lantern light.

We had chased after radio-collared geese
and photographed humpback whales
shoaling in the bay.

We had butchered our first deer
had rebuilt an outboard motor,
bathed in a Hobbit hole of a sauna

and kissed naked while the north wind
blew our towels off the boughs
and froze the hair on our bone-white skin.

This had been our precious world
twelve by sixteen feet
with seams taped up from the inside,

and it was gone
completely,
dissolved into the spongey wet moss, and the drip of rain.

No trace of the novel
I wrote in pencil
nor the letters we wrote home,

no trace of the arguments
or plans for the sumptuous
meals and long baths we would take in town,

no trace of how our memory
had burned a place in this cool
green world.

There was only a small pile

of firewood I had split before we left:
thick chunks of hemlock jumbled and slick

as uniform as a stack of bibles
and more readable
than anything

I have ever written.

four haiku from the year my parents died

Rain falling on snow.
　　Your dog has peed on the floor
waiting for his walk.

Wet cherry blossoms
　　fall on the parked cars all night,
in the morning . . . gone.

Sister cut lilacs
　　so we could smell them all day
cleaning out your house.

After last night's storm,
　　lonely on the great green lawn:
one bright red poppy.

six epithalamions and a
birth announcement

on this shore where love is not enough

for Nick and Julia

Waiting at the ferry dock for the boat to come
it occurs to you that it's always someone else
responsible for the wait.
It's always the complications at the other end of the line.
A ferryman walks between the cars
talking into a radio saying something about delays.

"You can't push a string," someone told you once
and you think, "Oh yeah? I could freeze it. I could straighten it out and
    push that sucker clear through a wall if I needed to."
You tap your steering wheel
then fuss with the radio to see if there is some news
of what's happening out there,
out there, where your future is balling up
in a tangled clump.

But once on the boat you go up on deck
and watch someone flying a kite off the stern.
You stand at the rail, watch the sea
spilling out to the sky and you think:
"This . . . right here. This is the world where love may be enough."
You don't even recall taking
a romantic stance at the rail, your hair blown back.
You hardly notice your new inward
and outward stare toward the horizon.
You close your eyes and catch yourself drifting
on the currents of the world,
like the kite above the widening V of your own wake
and you know there is nothing else
to do but unwind that frozen string
your heart has become.

When the ferry boat docks, you think, "Maybe I'll stay on.
Just ride back and forth the rest of my life."
Then you look around and not surprisingly
there are lots of you there, with your thoughts fluttering
among the scoters and herring gulls,

riding out towards the rippled horizon
broken only by islands
and pennanted boats, like bathtub toys.
You try and remember that boy or girl you first loved
back in third grade and you miss the call to return to your vehicle.
The ferryman talks into his radio
saying something about delays.

II.

Today we all came across
and arrived on this shore
with the smell of ocean
like confetti in our hair.
We are filled with love
and our hearts are like kites
untethered.
But this marriage we see today is not a ferry ride
and not one of these lovers is the anchor
and the other the kite.
They are too wise for that
and too settled now.

In the courthouse everyone comes aggrieved:
the families from trailer courts,
and gated cul-de-sacs,
the lovers who have entangled themselves in some
brutal drama, only want relief.
They want the extra weight their life has taken on
to be lifted.

In the courthouse the goddess holds a scale:
a string balanced in the center holds two trays
equally distant
equally balanced.
Both are kites
both are anchors
and the goddess is blindfolded so as not to jinx the deal.

For you can't push a string
and each of us who tries becomes entangled
and each of us always tries.

The ferryman talks into his radio
speaking of delays
and this is what he says:
"You can't stay here
you have to move on.
I don't make the rules.
I just know, that on this shore
there is enough love
and that love is not enough."

the map and territory of love

for Serena and Sam

Through the clouds the ground unscrolls
as a gigantic map, hard to read.
Those cold rivers sliding
through mounded hills and toy towns
are of vague interest,
but of no real relevance.
You might look over the top of a magazine
and watch a tired woman scold
a baby too young to understand and think,
"She shouldn't do that."

And when you land far from home
the ground, although closer,
is no easier to understand.
Whole watersheds blur through the windshield.
Trees and phone poles
sputter past, mostly unnoticed.
"Where can I drop you?"
you might say to the person reading a paper
in the backseat.

Sometimes our past can seem like that:
All of our ancestors,
ladders splining back through time,
Aunts and Uncles,
Parents gone or somehow missing
all whisper just out of hearing.
Their voices press in on us
like our tight formal clothes.
We want to address them somehow,
the great, great-grandparents
and the cousins gone lost in the war.
We reach out to those we never even knew
yet cannot find them
through all of this distance.

But not today.
Today a bride's slipper scuffs across gravel
and the groom's polished leather shoe
bends blades of grass with each step.
A woman in a blue organdy dress will cry,
someone's uncle will laugh,
and a friend who cut himself shaving might look away
just at the wrong time
to follow a bird out of sight
and miss everything.

For today, each moment is prickly with detail
and can only be made sensible by love.
A man, a woman combed and dressed
to perfection,
walk this short path.
"Here we all are," their presence says
and the bird comes back,
and all of the missing
snap to attention
having just located themselves among us
in the actual territory of love.

the way through

for Kari and Ben

"You ask the way to Cold Mountain?
There is no way through."
—Han Shan

Cold Mountain, Mount Tam,
Heart's Pass,
the future:
there is no way through.

Standing above the Namib desert
you thought you had solved
the puzzle your life had become:
blown sand billowing upward,
scooping and mounding,
covering everything
as if this violent world could emerge
once again, brand new and trackless
and you knew it was useless
trying to play your life
like a game of chess:
making one move, and then another.

The Great Barrier Reef,
traffic in San Francisco,
your job:
there is no way through.

Only a fine, attentive
love makes the world sacred
and you knew that then
standing on that African ridge
thinking that there is no loneliness
like finding yourself
fully inside your life and still
looking for that door.

There are no doors,
no steps,
no hammers nor saws
with which to gain entrance.

There is only this:
the turbulence of her breath
in and out,
both of your hearts beating
(just as they are right now)
each pulse the first
each pulse the last
each one as if it had never existed,
lasting forever
and fading away
just like a desert,
or a mountain
or this very moment
when you find yourselves
in the shelter of the sacred world
and wonder
just how it was
you ever found
your way through.

when the lights come up

for Marti and Jeff

After the film is over and the credits have run,
there is a moment in the dark when
our lives hover above us:
the tail of film is flapping off the reel
and the tired projectionist reaches for the houselights.

It's only then our lives seep back in,
first through our clothes then gradually through our skin
and we awaken, a little embarrassed
among all the others sitting there,
now, somehow, so small,
and forlorn.

Plato said that this was the human condition,
more than that, he taught
that the shadows were as close to the truth
as we were likely to come.
Not even the popcorn, the gum under the seats
nor the spilled sodas grabbing our shoes
are of consequence,
only the shadows on the wall, he said,
are the fabric of this flickering dream we promote
to each other as reality.

And he may be right
for when the lights come up
what we have here is the unfocused and unsorted
wide-angle view,
the hodge-podge of the actual.
Here is obesity and drunkenness,
here are the flaws of all our parents
twining down through the coupling of genes
come to rest in the soft flesh of our inconstant bodies.
Here is actual death,
rarely dramatic, but slow and bedridden,
where we never say the right thing
and when the lights come up
we are somehow gone.

Sometimes, in our lives we run out of a story,
and the lights come up on a brand-new scene:
Here are the live oak trees
and the tang of sage and ocean.
Here is lemon sunlight on a world
so vastly complex it makes a mockery of our
most vivid imaginations.
Who could predict this moment in a grove of trees
or the trillions of intricate moves
it takes to make just one day like this one?

For this is what Plato may have missed:
the shadows were a distraction,
the real show was the cave itself,
the stink of mud and the soft leathery wings
of bats breathing out toward the moonlight
out past the hole behind the waterfall
out past the mists on diamond cobwebs
out past the entrance
to where the brightening world awaits.

For we could not love so well
if the shadows were all there were,
we could not eat our fill at weddings
or hold hands in the movies.
We could not drink or flirt or dance
or celebrate loving one another if this
were all an inconstant flicker.

And even though we are always in costume, this moment,
this beginning, is all that is real.
This love, this air, which passes through the trees and
makes its last sweep through a bride's hair,
is all there is,
even death cannot still this wind
even death cannot invade our solemnity
on this day,
at this hour
when we love one another
and step through this fading light
into the unwritten story line
which is all we will ever know.

accidental blessings

for Lisa Busch and Davy Lubin

"Others have come in their slow way into
my thought, and some have tried to help or to hurt:
ask me what difference their strongest
love or hate has made . . .

What the river says, that is what I say."
—*Ask Me* by William Stafford

On the afternoon he died,
Bill Stafford wrote a note to his wife
on the back of a photograph.
He was at his desk,
feeling fine, his friends later said.
"I have always loved you,"
he wrote on the picture of her
taken some forty years before.
Then he lay down.

Dorothy poked into the berries
and the blades of the blender bit the spoon
spattering red pulp around the room
"Bill? . . . Bill?" she said. "Can you come help me?"
But of course he couldn't.

That this life is a collision of accidental blessings
makes it no less precious or determined.
We know the water rises from the oceans
is blown against the mountains
then drops down into streams but
remember, there is no sense in this
and none of the rules that come after
matter to those frantic, falling waters.

This is anarchy,
this blessing of rain.
This is what your love is
and what we are here to celebrate:
the lucky, unexpected meeting that somehow comes to ground.

So, this is what the river says:
Rain and rock, our souls
the voice of grasses on the bank
dipper and junco, each moment
filling the cup of right now
each kiss a small sip
mud and dying fish
bears and smolts
trout and bushes
salmonberry
blueberry
huckleberry
nagoonberry
thimbleberry
cloudberry
enough pure sweetness in this life
to compensate for anything,
anything, including death.

And this, my dear friends, is what I say:
in this wet country love may not always be enough
but eventually
it will fill everything left open.

before you were born this was everything i knew about you

Once, on a brown picnic table
there was a cup left out
with a drop of mint tea
and a spider in the bottom.
I took the cup and wiped it out
with my finger, setting the spider on the edge
of the damp table to watch it escape
into the crack between the boards
then, forgetting what I was doing,
I licked the sweet tea off of my finger.

I thought of you then
and even tried to say your name,
but it would be months
before we were to be introduced.

This then, was my premonition
and I wrote it down:
the spider, the cup
the fine grit of autumn
stuck, like your name,
on the tip of my tongue,
like getting to be alive
more than twice.

ephemera

for Joselyn and Will

A file of photos arrive,
and I shake the contents
out on my lap:
children with dogs in bathtubs
and a man in a hat standing next
to a Studebaker station wagon,
teenagers with rods and strings of trout
bright as money.

But what connects them:
a Polaroid of a birthday party
a girl in pigtails and thick glasses,
young ones dressed as Zoro
or lions,
or in soccer shorts
and shin guards
hands draped carelessly
around the shoulders of their
comrades long forgotten?

You will have a file like this someday:
a shot of the girl in the Field Museum
with magnets in her eyes,
children putting up a Christmas tree
in the den where they usually did not play,
the pink of their nightgowns the same
as the bubble gum they chewed
and blew into ornament-sized bubbles.

We will be in that file.
All of us in our nice clothes,
faces fluttering out
like handfuls of falling leaves
the connections between us
invisible
or gone:
aunts, uncles

parents and cousins
just as young as we are right now
but somehow already ancestors
in the whir and snap of a shutter.

There is a scrap of paper somewhere
that I wish I had tonight:
two words in French
written from a hospital bed
a few days after you were born.
The surgeons let your father in to see her;
the web of her brain torn by a stroke.
She could not speak but had lived through the night
and when he handed her a piece of paper
not knowing what she could say
she returned it with only this:
"Je t'aime," she wrote
in the French she learned in school.
I love you.

And now we are all here;
witnesses to this happiness
and all we really know is this:
that everything we save in bags,
or on the shelves of the houses we will buy and sell,
all of it is ephemera,
the knitted web of our existence
held together
by a love
as fine as the track of an electrical impulse
through the brain
or as fragile as an old photograph
made of nothing but light.

"Je t'aime"
your mother wrote
and in that is the connection
between these things:
a bride and groom,
all of us in one place
for this lucky instant when
the shutter clicks
and everything else
in this bright world
moves on.